Economics Through the Looking Glass

The Distorted Perspective of The New Palgrave Dictionary of Economics

MARK BLAUG

University of London and
University of Buckingham

Institute of Economic Affairs
1988

First published in June 1988

by

THE INSTITUTE OF ECONOMIC AFFAIRS

2 Lord North Street, Westminster, London SW1P 3LB

© The Institute of Economic Affairs 1988

Occasional Paper 78

ISSN 0073-909X

ISBN 0-255 36212-9

Printed in Great Britain by

GORON PRO-PRINT CO LTD, LANCING, WEST SUSSEX

Set in Berthold Plantin 11 on 12 point

Economics Through the Looking Glass

MARK BLAUG

Summary

1. The *New Palgrave Dictionary of Economics* seeks to encompass the academic discipline of economics in four volumes and over four million words of text and symbols.

2. According to the editors, their aim was to provide the student of economics with an easily accessibly overview of economics.

3. As a work of scholarship the *New Palgrave Dictionary* possesses several major flaws which greatly damage this claim and undermine the requirement of any reference work: that it give an unbiased and scholarly account of key terms and concepts.

4. The editors of Palgrave are disciples of an obscure School of Economic Thought (so-called Sraffian economics). They have, according to Professor Blaug, sought to advance their view of economics without clearly acknowledging its shortcomings and the fact that it does not accord with mainstream economics.

5. The New Palgrave when read from cover to cover conveys a idiosyncratic and biased view of modern economics mainly through the commissioning of highly tendentious contributions on central economic concepts. The dictionary is more accurately described as the 'Marxian/Sraffian Dictionary of Theoretical Economics'.

6. The editors have not sought to ensure that each entry is balanced, but have relied on other entries to provide counter or different analyses of the same topic. This creates confusion and decreases substantially the utility of the Dictionary as a work of reference.

7. The high degree of mathematical competence required to comprehend some entries also serves to obscure the contribution of economics in key areas, such as international trade, and re-inforces the editors' view that theoretical economics devoid of empirical content defines the core of the subject and is sufficient to generate fundamental insights into the working of the real economy.

Occasional Paper 78 is published (price £3·50) by

THE INSTITUTE OF ECONOMIC AFFAIRS
2 Lord North Street, Westminster
London SW1P 3LB   Telephone: 01-799 3745

IEA PUBLICATIONS
Subscription Service

An annual subscription is the most convenient way to obtain our publications. Every title we produce in all our regular series will be sent to you immediately on publication and without further charge, representing a substantial saving.

Individual subscription rates*

Britain:
£25·00 p.a. including postage.
£23·00 p.a. if paid by Banker's Order.
£15·00 p.a. to teachers and students who pay *personally*.

Europe:
£25·00 p.a. including postage.

South America:
£35·00 p.a. or equivalent.

Other Countries:
Rates on application. In most countries subscriptions are handled by local agents. Addresses are available from the IEA.

* These rates are *not* available to companies or to institutions.

To: The Treasurer, Institute of Economic Affairs,
2 Lord North Street, Westminster,
London SW1P 3LB

I should like to subscribe from ....

I enclose a cheque/postal order for:

☐ £25·00

☐ £15·00   I am a teacher/student at ....

....

☐ Please send a Banker's Order form.

☐ Please send an invoice.

☐ Please charge my credit card:

Please tick   ☐ *VISA*   ☐ 🅰   ☐ AMERICAN EXPRESS   ☐ Ⓞ

Card No: ☐☐☐☐☐☐☐☐☐☐☐☐☐☐☐☐☐☐☐

In addition I would like to purchase the following previously published titles: *BLOCK LETTERS PLEASE*

....

....

Name ....

Address ....

....

.... Post Code ....

Signed .... Date ....

OP78

Contents

FOREWORD .. .. *Cento Veljanovski* 5

THE AUTHOR 9

I INTRODUCTION 11
   New Palgrave Editors are Anti-Neo-Classical .. 12
   A Sraffian Trio ... A Tendentious Dictionary .. 14
   'Curious Results' 15
   Mathematics and All That.. 17
   Gold Amidst the Dross 18

II WHAT IS SRAFFIAN ECONOMICS? 21
   Constant-Cost Supply Curve 24
   'Beautiful Technical Puzzles' 26
   Re-interpreting History 27

III MARXIAN ECONOMICS 29

IV KEYNESIAN ECONOMICS 31

V THE SWITCHING DEBATE 32
   Exceptions Prove the Rule! 33
   Mid-air Economics 34

VI GENERAL EQUILIBRIUM THEORY 35
   Proof not Practice 35
   Competition as Outcome Rather than Process .. 36
   Abstraction or Description? 37

VII BACK TO SRAFFA 39
   Theory Without Relevance 40

VIII METHODOLOGY 42
       Limitations of Econometric Models 43
       Rhetoric or Verification? 44

 IX MORE METHODOLOGY 45

  X CONCLUSION 46

BIBLIOGRAPHICAL REFERENCES 49

TABLES
  1: Genuinely Fresh Entries 19
  2: Omitted Topics 20
  3: Entries on Marxian Economics 30

FIGURES
  1: Constant Returns to Scale 23
  2: Long- and Short-run Average Costs 25

SUMMARY .. .. *Back cover*

[4]

Foreword

IT IS a reason for rejoicing when a reputable publisher, three ambitious editors and nearly 900 hundred contributors, many amongst the most eminent economists in the profession, join forces to produce what is in the publisher's estimation a magisterial overview of the academic discipline of economics. This work goes under the title of *The New Palgrave Dictionary of Economics*[1] – containing over four million words and symbols in a tightly packed text housed in four volumes. It is an enterprise which draws from an earlier attempt – *Palgrave's Dictionary of Political Economy* edited by Inglis Palgrave and first published by Macmillan in 1894. With periodic updating *The New Palgrave*, while not likely to be the last word in economics, could well become an indispensable source of ready reference for the student of economics, especially in the light of the explosion of articles and books in the subject over the last two decades.

It is for these reasons that the Institute of Economic Affairs decided to commission Professor Mark Blaug, of the University of London and the University of Buckingham, to give his views on *The New Palgrave*. Professor Blaug is eminently qualified to undertake this assignment. He is a prominent and highly regarded interpreter of developments in economics and his *Economic Theory in Retrospect*[2] is regarded by many as a classic. Professor Blaug has approached his task with gusto and industry. He can claim, without fear of contradiction, to be one of the few people in the world to have read each of the four volumes of *The New Palgrave* from cover to cover. He is therefore in a unique position to evaluate the entirety of *The New Palgrave* and not, like most reviewers, from a random sample of entries.

The New Palgrave Dictionary seeks to provide a reference work which can be dipped into by student, teacher, layman and

[1] J. Eatwell, M. Milgate, P. Newman (eds.), *The New Palgrave: A Dictionary of Economics*, 4 vols., London: Macmillan, 1987.

[2] Cambridge: Cambridge University Press, 4th edn. 1985.

[5]

professional economist. The editors (John Eatwell, Murray Milgate and Peter Newman) claim that their aim is identical to that stated in the preface to the first edition of the original *Palgrave*: namely, 'to provide the student with such assistance as may enable him to understand the position of economic thought at the present time'. Yet the editors of *The New Palgrave* have not sought to provide a balanced view of their subject. Rather they encouraged 'diversity and vivacity' through multiple entries on the same subject. These two objectives are not at all mutually consistent. Despite cross-referencing (which Professor Blaug notes is not really up to the task), the reader will never be sure whether what is read is 'balanced' or a one-sided story to be matched with an entry elsewhere presenting another view. And in any case, the high level of mathematical competence required to understand some entries on central topics places the dictionary beyond the grasp of both student and the generalist economist.

The editors of *The New Palgrave* throw down a challenge: 'the reader will find that [it] is unbiased, in almost every sense of the word'. Professor Blaug strongly disagrees. His assessment of the contents of the enterprise is not favourable and gives rise to considerable concern. He argues that the tone, emphasis, the way the editorial 'knife' has cut and the selection of key entries have produced a work that is distinctly biased and incomplete. In short, the Dictionary is perhaps better entitled, for reasons which will become abundantly obvious from his text, the *Marxian/ Sraffian Dictionary of Theoretical Economics*.

Professor Blaug's major disagreement with *The New Palgrave* is its treatment of crucial topics in economics and the way the editors have draped economics in a particular uniform not worn by many economists. Professor Blaug's criticisms are far from the familiar game of academic sniping. As he is quick to point out, some entries are gems, others excellent treatments of the subject, but many are just incomprehensible to other than the *cognoscenti* (which may number only their author) and some simply un-balanced, utterly idiosyncratic and downright distorted.

Economics is a subject which is tolerant of many different schools and divergent views, particulary of the policy impli-cations to be drawn from its core theory. Indeed, since economics is not a 'profession' it has not operated as a closed shop. Many times economics has been torn by deep intellectual controversy and massive policy differences. But there is among the overwhelming majority of economists, and by this I mean well over 90 per cent, a core of theory which all learn and which defines the subject. This theory, called neo-classical economics, views man, whether he operates individually in the market-place or in the firm, family and/or any other institution, as a rational maximiser of his self-chosen ends. Without acceptance of this central behavioural tenet, I would argue, no useful economic generalisations, such as are provided by the basic laws of supply and demand, can be made.

Professor Blaug has convincingly argued that *The New Palgrave* gives a distorted picture of economics derived from a peculiar and idiosyncratic school of economics – so-called 'Sraffian economics'. I will leave it to Professor Blaug's pungent and vigorous discussion to highlight the subtle ways that *The New Palgrave* in its totality distorts the core of economics and elevates out of all proportion to its importance and acceptability among fellow economists the theoretical prognostications of perhaps a handful of academics at Cambridge University and several provincial Italian universities. If the view espoused in *The New Palgrave* were accepted by economic theorists, then the whole edifice of economics built upon market analysis from Adam Smith on, would come crashing down. In 1974 Professor Blaug wrote a thorough and widely-read critique of Sraffian economics for the IEA entitled *The Cambridge Revolution: Success or Failure?*[1] There he concluded on the criticisms and alternative theories advanced by Cambridge economists of the same ilk as the editors of *The New Palgrave*, that 'whatever is wrong with neo-classical economics (and who can doubt that there is much to complain of?), it wins hands down on all possible criteria' compared with Sraffian economics. Here he returns and warms to this theme.

The Institute of Economic Affairs dissociates itself from the analysis and conclusions of its authors. Professor Blaug's discussion is an erudite, considered and highly-informed evaluation of an important work. It therefore promotes the IEA's principal objective, faithfully pursued for the last three

---

[1] Hobart Paperback No. 6, 2nd edn., 1975.

decades,[1] of advancing knowledge of economics. The reader cannot but be struck by the wit and verve with which Professor Blaug has approached his chosen task. It is a tribute to his scholarship that he has read *The New Palgrave* and has felt moved to evaluate it for the Institute in such frank terms. A debt of gratitude is owed to Arthur Seldon for his extensive and detailed comments on an earlier draft, and his enthusiasm for this venture. I commend this *Occasional Paper* to all who want a fresh insight into economic theory and its controversies which affect the discipline of economics.

May 1988   CENTO VELJANOVSKI

[1] The reader is also referred to Arthur Seldon's 'The Eatwell-Milgate-Newman Dictionary – Enlightenment or Ideology?', *Economic Affairs*, Vol. 8, No. 4, April/May 1988, pp. 42-46.

The Author

MARK BLAUG was born in the Netherlands in 1927 and educated there until the war. He came to England in 1940 and was subsequently evacuated to the United States in 1942. He attended high school and college in New York, obtaining an MA in 1952 and PhD in Economics in 1955 at Columbia University.

He worked as a statistician for the US Department of Labour and then joined the staff of Yale University in 1954 as an Assistant Professor of Economics, where he remained until 1962. He was Visiting Professor in the History of Economic Thought at the University of Manchester, 1960-61, Visiting Professor in the Economics of Education at the University of Chicago, 1965-66, Professor of the Economics of Education at the University of London Institute of Education, 1969-84, and is now Professor Emeritus at the University of London and Consultant Professor of Economics at the University of Buckingham. He is also a Director of Edward Elgar Publishing Ltd.

He was Simon B. Guggenheim Foundation Fellow, 1958-59, and Social Science Research Council Faculty Research Fellow, 1962-63; consultant to UNESCO, OECD, World Bank, ILO and the Ford Foundation; lived in India in 1967, in Thailand in 1969, and has participated in a large number of international missions to developing countries in Asia and Africa.

He is the author of *Economic Theory in Retrospect* (4th edn., 1985), *Introduction to the Economics of Education* (1970), *Education and the Employment Problem in Developing Countries* (1973), *The Methodology of Economics* (1980), *Great Economists Since Keynes* (1985), *Great Economists Before Keynes* (1986) and *Economic History and the History of Economics* (1986).

For the IEA he has previously written *The Cambridge Revolution: Success or Failure?* (Hobart Paperback No. 6, 1974, 2nd (revised) edn. 1975).

Economics Through the Looking Glass

MARK BLAUG

I

INTRODUCTION

THERE IS in economics, or at least among the overwhelming majority of its disciples, broad agreement as to what represents the corpus of their subject. This corpus revolves around the concept of maximising behaviour, whether it be by the individual, firm or institution. There are, of course, 'Schools' of economic thought which take a heterodox view of economics and some are openly and vociferously critical of neo-classical economics. Indeed internal controversy and challenges to a discipline are a sign of its vitality and are to be welcomed. However, these schools represent a minority fringe of intellectual activity. But when a group of academics, purporting to collect together a magisterial survey of economic knowledge, mistakes the fringe for the solid core of the discipline, whether overtly or by more subtle devices, then this is cause for concern. The New Palgrave Dictionary has been heralded as a major publishing event and like its predecessor has the potential to become an important part of the economist's library. Yet it fails to supply the teacher, student and layman with a balanced overview of economics today. It is, to be perfectly frank, an idiosyncratic work. In this *Occasional Paper* I take the opportunity to expose the nature of the biases and deficiencies of the New Palgrave based on a full reading of its four volumes and over four million words.

The first 'Palgrave' Dictionary of Economics was published in three volumes almost a century ago by R. H. Inglis Palgrave, then editor of *The Economist*. It was called a dictionary but it was really an encyclopedia of economics, the first compendium of its kind in English. It was a highly uneven work but it did contain numerous entries by some of England's leading contemporary economists and its major biographical articles instantly became classical references. It was re-edited in the 1920s by Henry Higgs but the rise of monopolistic competition theory and the Keynesian Revolution soon rendered even that edition obsolete. By the 1950s economic theory had moved so rapidly in a mathematical and econometric direction that both the original and the re-edited Palgrave were hardly of interest to economists without a training in the history of economic thought. The masterly and comprehensive *International Encyclopedia of the Social Sciences*, edited by David L. Sills and published in 17 volumes in 1968 (with a biographical supplement in 1979), devoted something like a quarter of its 10,000 pages to economics. It took stock of new developments in the subject and continues to this day to serve as a major reference work in economics.

Nevertheless, there was much talk all through the 1970s of an Encyclopedia of Economics that would update and extend the treatment of economics in the Sills encyclopedia. Macmillan, the publisher of both Palgrave and Sills, considered at least two American proposals for such an encyclopedia and finally decided in 1983 to launch a New Palgrave. For its editors, they chose John Eatwell, Murray Milgate and Peter Newman.[1]

New Palgrave Editors are Anti-Neo-Classical

This was a strange choice in at least two senses: none of the three editors is American and yet the subject of economics is nowadays overwhelmingly dominated by Americans; moreover, none of the three editors believes in mainstream or so-called 'neo-classical' economics and two of them are in print as rejecting it root and branch. John Eatwell is a Fellow and Lecturer in Economics at Trinity College, Cambridge, co-author with Joan Robinson of an off-beat textbook, *An Introduction to Modern Economics* (1973),[2] and the presenter of the BBC-TV series *Whatever Happened to Britain?* (1982).[3] He is a post-Keynesian and neo-Ricardian economist, a follower of Nicholas Kaldor when it

---

[1] J. Eatwell, M. Milgate, P. Newman (eds.), *The New Palgrave: A Dictionary of Economics*, 4 vols., London: Macmillan, 1987, pp. 979, 1,044, 1,085, 1,025.

[2] London: McGraw-Hill.   [3] London: Duckworth for the BBC.

comes to the ills of the British economy and a disciple of Piero Sraffa in the higher reaches of economic theory. Murray Milgate, one-time student of Eatwell and now Associate Professor at Harvard University, is the author of *Capital and Employment* (1982),[1] a book which aspires to combine Keynes' theory of income determination with Sraffa's theory of value and distribution.[2] Peter Newman of Johns Hopkins University (but British born and British educated) is a mathematical economist who has also worked on the demographic problems of developing countries. He would seem at first glance to belong to a wholly different school of thought from Eatwell and Milgate. But in fact Newman's early article-review of Sraffa's *Production of Commodities by Means of Commodities* (1960) proved to be extremely influential for the burgeoning Sraffa Industry.[3] In short, even Newman is a Sraffian of sorts.

Whatever we may think of the validity and significance of the economics of Sraffa (more of that anon), it is a fact that Sraffians are a tiny minority among modern economists. Apart from the Universities of Cambridge and Manchester and two or three polytechnics, it is difficult to round up more than a dozen Sraffians in Britain. There are hardly any in America's 3,000 institutions of higher learning. The real centre of the Sraffa School is in Italy – for no better reason than that Sraffa was Italian (even though he spent almost his entire adult life at Cambridge). The leadership of the Sraffa 'Church' in Italy is shared between Sraffa's literary executor, Piero Garegnani of the University of Rome, and Luigi Pasinetti of the Universita Cattolica del Sacro Cuore in Milan; but there are dozens of enthusiastic followers in many Italian universities – of whom 16 appear in this dictionary – and the 'house' journal of the

[1] London: Macmillan.

[2] Eatwell and Milgate also edited a collection of papers, *Keynes's Economics and the Theory of Value and Distribution* (London: Duckworth, 1983), which exemplifies the same aim.

[3] P. Newman, 'Production of Commodities by Means of Commodities', *Schweizerische Zeitschrift für Volkswirtschaft und Statistik*, 98, March 1962. Newman showed that Sraffa's ideas could be neatly expounded with the aid of certain properties of non-negative square matrices traditionally associated with the names of Perron and Frobenius, two German mathematicians of the early years of this century, since when all Sraffian economics has come to be written in terms of Perron-Frobenius algebra.

Sraffians, *Political Economy, Studies in the Surplus Approach*, is published twice a year in Turin. In the rest of Europe and elsewhere in Asia, Africa and Latin America, it may be possible to collect another five or six self-declared Sraffians but not many more than that.

A Sraffian Trio ... A Tendentious Dictionary

To have invited three Sraffians to edit a new Palgrave dictionary of economics is roughly equivalent to asking three atheists to edit an encyclopedia of Christianity: it is conceivable that such a trio would carry out its task with studious impartiality, but it is not very likely. And, indeed, it has not come to pass in this case. The New Palgrave is a tendentious work that fails to reflect the mainstream of orthodox doctrine in economics and that does not even do justice to the entire range of dissenting and heterodox opinion.

The editors clearly saw The New Palgrave as a signal opportunity to put their particular views on the map. At the same time, they were aware that a dictionary of economics along entirely Sraffian lines would not be commercially viable. They solved this problem with characteristic *chutzpah*. Instead of attempting to present a balanced account of controversial issues in economics, including a frank admission of certain fundamental methodological and ideological disagreements among members of the profession, they simply let a thousand flowers bloom, leaving it to the reader to separate the perennials from the weeds. As they say in their preface:

'On many non-biographical subjects, we have tried to capture diversity and vivacity of views by having multiple entries, under similar but different titles. In this way we hoped to obtain essays that present the results and methods of research with fairness and accuracy, but not necessarily from a "balanced" point of view. Such a view in these cases should be sought externally, as it were, using the system of cross-references to consult other relevant entries. This means more work for the reader but should yield correspondingly greater reward.' (I: ix)

Do the four volumes of The New Palgrave represent 'the results and methods of research with fairness and accuracy', if not necessarily from 'a "balanced" point of view'? Not when the results and methods touch on what Sraffians regard as sensitive issues, such as, for example, the ideas of Ricardo, Marx, Keynes and Sraffa himself. In the entire 4,100 pages and over 4 million words of The New Palgrave there is a large number of extremely sympathetic and even adulatory expositions of Marxian economics but there is not one single critical account of any of Marx's ideas (with the possible exception of Ernst Gellner on the Economic Interpretation of History, II: 47-51). Similarly, there are some 50 expositions of Sraffian economics under various headings but only two entries, namely, my own on Classical Economics (I: 434-44) and Paul Samuelson's on Sraffian Economics (IV: 452-60), which even begin to entertain the possibility that Sraffa's words may not represent the alpha and omega of economics. A sample count of pages in The New Palgrave shows that Marx and Sraffa are quoted more frequently, indeed, much more frequently, than Adam Smith, Alfred Marshall, Leon Walras, Maynard Keynes, Kenneth Arrow, Milton Friedman, Paul Samuelson or whoever you care to name. This indicates a lack of balance in the dictionary which appears elsewhere in the length of entries devoted to certain topics, to the very choice of titles for some entries, and even to the selection of the more than 900 economists who agreed to contribute.

'Curious Results'

The Eatwell-Milgate-Newman policy of publishing multiple entries with slightly different titles for identical subjects constantly produces curious results, in which the outcome of the study of any topic depends principally on the reader's tenacity in following up all the cross-references (placed oddly at the end of the articles). To give two examples, Charles Goodhart in an essay on the Monetary Base denies categorically that the supply of money is an exogenous variable, that is to say that the monetary authorities are able to increase or decrease the money supply at will (III: 50). But Karl Brunner in an entry on Money Supply, the third reference cited at the end of Goodhart's article, equally categorically insists the very opposite: 'the monetary authorities can effectively control the money stock' (III: 528). This is a famous bone of contention about 'monetarism', because if Goodhart is right, monetarism is a nonsense. Now, there is nothing wrong on the face of it with either argument (there is a pertinent entry here by Meghnad Desai on Endogenous and Exogenous Money, II: 136-7), but a good editor would have invited both authors to refer to each other's diametrically opposed viewpoints, or else would have ensured such a cross-reference editorially. Similarly, Alan Peacock extols Economic Freedom (II: 33-5) as freedom for the individual; whereas C. B. Macpherson castigates Individualism (II: 75-7) as the ideology of the bourgeoisie, but the two essays are not cross-referenced to each other – almost as if the editors failed to realise that economic freedom *is* individualism. It would be easy to give many more instances of this sort of confusion arising from unannounced conflicts of opinion in multiple entries on identical subjects. On balance, a policy of presenting competing opinions under the *same* title would have been vastly preferable to the Eatwell-Milgate-Newman policy of several entries under *different* titles on what is in fact one and the same topic.

The New Palgrave is avowedly a dictionary of economic theories and doctrines (I: ix). There are indeed articles on institutions such as Auctions (I: 138-44) and Financial Intermediaries (II: 340-8), and Robert Heilbroner and Alec Nove write on Capitalism and Socialism (I: 347-53, IV: 398-407), each with equal vigour and sceptical disdain of standard opinion on these explosive institutional topics. But The New Palgrave is clearly not the place to go for descriptions of how the World Bank operates or how different countries regulate the pricing policies of public utilities. Accepting this limitation and hence the focus on questions of economic theory, The New Palgrave nevertheless demonstrates an almost shocking disregard for students, journalists, writers, politicians and lay readers. The original Palgrave was addressed to 'the student with such assistance as may enable him to understand the position of economic thought at the present time'. But this New Palgrave is unhesitatingly addressed to the professional economist. The level of analytical competence required to read many of the entries on even such standard topics as demand, supply and equilibrium is forbiddingly high, and all the mathematical essays sail upwards into the stratosphere of algebraic topology, optimal control theory and dynamic programming without so much as a consoling word for undergraduates whose mathematics does not extend much beyond differential calculus and linear algebra.

[16]

Now, obviously, modern economics is an increasingly mathematical subject and, equally obviously, any encyclopedia of modern economics must contain an account of recent developments in mathematical economics, as well as much economics mathematically treated. But to have allowed John Chipman to write 30,000 words – a thick pamphlet or a small book and the longest entry in the volume – on International Trade (II: 922-52) with no concessions to the 'average' literary economist, not to mention the mythical 'general reader', amounts to an abnegation of editorial responsibility.[1] This brand of formalism, a revelling in technique for technique's sake, is certainly a feature of much modern economics; yet an encyclopedia of economics would hardly seem an appropriate place to advertise it. Entries like those of Stephen Robinson on Convex Programming (I: 647-59), William Parry on Ergodic Theory (II: 184-7), Richard Savage on Random Variables (IV: 54-64), and many more like it read like chapters in a textbook of advanced mathematical economics and statistics. One expects articles such as Duality by Peter Newman (I: 924-34), Lyapunov Function by Charles Henry (II: 256-9), Non-linear Programming by Michael Intriligator (III: 666-70), and Turnpike Theory by Lionel McKenzie (IV: 712-20) to be difficult – and they are – but it is not easy to see why essays on such standard topics as Aggregate Demand Theory by Hugo Sonnenschein (I: 47-50), Demand Theory by Volker Böhm and Hans Haller (I: 785-91), Financial Markets by Nils Hakansson (II: 351-4), and Perfect Competition by Ali Khan (III: 831-4) have to be presented in a style that makes them virtually unintelligible to those outside the coterie of mathematical economists.

The mind-boggling obscurity of many of the articles is part and parcel of the editors' master plan: its purpose is to dispel the worry that mainstream economists might otherwise have felt about a dictionary edited by three Sraffians. Mainstream economists are all too inclined to equate professional competence with a technically demanding style. Formalism has an iron grip

[1] Ian Steedman writes on 'Foreign Trade' (II: 406-11) in words and diagrams but his entry is not an account of the phenomenon of foreign trade but a critique of neo-classical trade theory from the standpoint of Sraffa and Cambridge capital theory. More to the point, however, is Comparative Advantage by Ronald Findlay (I: 514-7).

on much of modern economics: to be intelligible is to be suspect.[1] In short, in some quarters the high proportion of unreadable entries in The New Palgrave will be regarded as proof positive that high professional standards have been maintained.

Gold Amidst the Dross

With that caveat, there is nevertheless much in these volumes to praise. Clearly, with 2,000 entries, including 700 biographies, there are bound to be hits as well as misses. Some of the biographies of the great economists of the past are little masterpieces – Edgeworth by Peter Newman (II: 84-98), Fisher by James Tobin (II: 369-76), Malthus by John Pullen (III: 280-5), Marshall by John Whitaker (III: 350-63), Smith by Andrew Skinner (IV: 357-74), and Walras by Donald Walker (IV: 852-62) – but there are also striking biographies of living or recently deceased economists, such as Friedman by Alan Walters (II: 420-7), Kaldor by Adrian Wood (III: 3-8), Kalecki by Karl Laski (III: 8-14), Meade by David Vines (III: 400-6), and Joan Robinson by Luigi Pasinetti (IV: 212-7). In addition, there are hundreds of biographies of minor 20th-century economists, which are simply not available anywhere else.

Among the entries on various subjects, there are many that re-hearse analyses and arguments well-known from other sources. Ronald Jones is excellent on Heckscher-Ohlin trade theory (II: 520-7) but he has written so often on this theme elsewhere that the sense of discovery is gone – that is true of many other entries, such as Gerard Debreu on Existence of General Equilibrium (II: 216-9), Becker on the Family (II: 281-6), Wassily Leontief on Input-Output Analysis (II: 860-4), Don Patinkin on Keynes (III: 19-41), Gordon Tullock on Public Choice (III: 1,040-4), William Baumol on Ramsey Pricing (IV: 49-51), and Armatya Sen on Social Choice (IV: 382-93). That being said, I can recommend the entries in Table 1 as saying something new, or at least expressing it in a new form.

But my favourite single entry is the one on the Coase Theorem by Robert Cooter (I: 457-60), an explanation of one of the most profound and yet most misunderstood ideas in the whole of

[1] Collander and Klamer (1987) have shown that American postgraduate education in economics is thoroughly technique-ridden.

TABLE 1: **Genuinely Fresh Entries**

Entry	Author	Vol./Pages
Bayesian inference	Arnold Zellner	I: 208-18
Behavioural economics	Herbert Simon	I: 221-25
Biological application of economics	Gordon Tullock	I: 246-47
Co-determination and profit-sharing	Mario Nuti	I: 465-69
Division of labour	Peter Groenewegen	I: 901-06
Economic theory and the hypothesis of rationality	Kenneth Arrow	II: 69-74
Experimental methods in economics	Vernon Smith	II: 241-49
Game theory	Robert Aumann	II: 460-82
Equilibrium, development of concept	Murray Milgate	II: 178-82
Efficient market hypothesis	Burton Malkiel	II: 120-23
Hunting and gathering economies	Vernon Smith	II: 697-99
Neutrality of money	Don Patinkin	III: 639-45
Paradoxes	Neil de Marchi	III: 796-99
New classical macro-economics	Stanley Fisher	III: 647-50
Pareto-efficiency	Brian Lockwood	III: 811-13
Probability	Ian Hacking	III: 977-83
Quantity theory of money	Milton Friedman	IV: 3-19
Rent control	Kurt Klappholz	IV: 143-45
Real-cost doctrine	John Maloney	IV: 103-04
Second best	Peter Böhm	IV: 280-83
Statistical inference	D. V. Lindley	IV: 490-93
Welfare economics	Allan Feldman	IV: 889-94

welfare economics. The Coase Theorem is the proposition that 'market failure' due to externalities in either production or consumption can sometimes, and perhaps even frequently, be cured by a mere change in legal entitlements; in that case what is required to cure the ills of the market is not government intervention but a change in property laws. Cooter unpacks this theorem and demonstrates elegantly that it is at best a quarter-truth.

In other words, there is much gold amidst the dross but on

TABLE 2: **Omitted Topics**

Automation	Mixed economy
Bank deposit multiplier	Occupational licensing
Debt management	On-the-job training
Director's Law (or its corollary, the median voter theorem)	Output budgeting
	Producer's surplus
Earnings differentials	Stages of growth
Empirical testing	State provision of education (there
Factors of production	is one on state provision of
Falsification	medical services)
Flexitime	Stock markets
Fringe benefits	Vacancies
Grants economics	Voucher schemes
Internal labour markets	Work sharing
Labour force participation rate	

balance, and particularly when read from cover to cover – which I can testify takes only four to five weeks if one gives up eating and sleeping – The New Palgrave conveys a slanted picture of modern economics. I say nothing about the omission of entries for many important topics (Table 2), and many recognised branches of economics – the Economics of Education (except as another term for human capital theory), Comparative Economic Systems, Cultural Economics, and the History of Economic Thought – despite the existence of professional journals exclusively devoted to each of these specialisations.[1] The index is of some help in locating a perfunctory reference to two or three of these omitted subjects, but in general the index is not to be trusted because it seems to have been prepared by computer using a list of key terms. Thus, if we are interested in the New

---

[1] There is an entry for Human Capital (II: 681-90), but this is only part, although a central part, of the economics of education. There is an entry for Performing Arts (III: 841-3), but again this is only an aspect of cultural economics. A glance at the contents of 'Current Periodicals' in the *Journal of Economic Literature* would have informed the editors of the existence of the *Economics of Education Review* and the *Journal of Cultural Economics*. The editors profess a great interest in viewing current economic ideas in historical perspective (I: x), yet they refuse to acknowledge the history of economic thought as a recognised field of specialisation. I admit to a personal concern about all three of these omissions.

Household Economics of Gary Becker, the index does nothing to relate separate references to the 'new household economics', 'household production', 'family', and 'fertility, determinants of', even though all these refer to one and the same complex of ideas. Similarly, the index cites 'Verdoorn's Law'[1] but does not refer to Kaldor's endorsement of it in all his later writings. Such examples of poor indexing could be multiplied almost indefinitely.

I shall also say nothing (or almost nothing) about occasional instances of editorial sloppiness, such as bibliographies entirely omitted or cut short in biographical entries or the inconsistent use of one or another system of referring to the secondary literature (I: 231, 266; II: 519, 569, 640, 666; III: 17, 60, 102, 131, 142, 218, 267, 301, 325, 362, 442, 814; IV: 228, 233, 245, 249, 259, 287, 350, 768, 770, 832) – only a petty mind like my own would even notice it. And being petty I cannot forego a comment on the irritatingly small print-size adopted by Macmillan in belated imitation of the original Palgrave (8 on 9 point Monotype Times in double columns); compare that to the magnificent and generous typeface of the *Sills International Encyclopedia of the Social Sciences*, which is always a visual pleasure to read. On the plus side, however, is the superb proof-reading of the Macmillan editor, Margot Levy. I found only 13 misprints in over 4,000 pages (I: 286, 331, 545, 570; II: 25, 642, 645, 657, 861; III: 55, 266, 442, 527, 782; IV: 494, 988), but only two of these (I: 286, III: 442) were serious.

II

WHAT IS SRAFFIAN ECONOMICS?

THE NEW PALGRAVE is designed, as we have said, to promote Sraffian economics. But what is Sraffian economics? This is not the place for yet another exposition of the Sraffian system but it is worth spending some time describing the flavour and the

[1] Verdoorn's Law is the finding that the productivity of labour depends on the rate of growth of an industry; in consequence, growth breeds more growth in the same way that success breeds success. Kaldor based his theory of manufacturing as the engine of an economy's growth on Verdoorn's Law.

upshot of Sraffa's slim volume with the strange title, *Production of Commodities by Means of Commodities* (1960).[1]

Sraffa's book contains no introduction or conclusion but it does carry the intriguing subtitle: 'prelude to a critique of economic theory'. From various hints in the book, the economic theory in question appears to be the whole of the post-1870 marginalist or neo-classical tradition. According to this tradition, goods and services as well as the factors of production are determined in the first instance by demand and supply and ultimately by the pattern of consumer preferences, the prevailing techniques of production and the ownership of productive factors among individual economic agents, that is, tastes, technology and endowments. Sraffa proceeds to criticise this type of theorising by claiming that it is perfectly possible to explain the determination of relative prices by technology alone without any reference to consumer demand. However, this technology must preclude substitution among the factors of production in response to changing wage and interest rates; it must be technically rigid or, in the language of input-output analysis, it must be of the fixed-coefficients variety, that is, so many workers per ton of steel, so many spades per bushel of corn, and so on. Now, we all learned in school that to solve a system of simultaneous equations, you need at least as many equations as unknowns, and it is a simple mathematical fact that a set of *known* fixed-coefficients do not give us enough equations to determine the value of all the *unknown* prices in the economy. Thus, to determine prices, we have to assume something besides the technical structure of production, and that something is either the real wage-rate of labour (assuming there is only one kind of labour) or the uniform rate of profit on capital.

Suppose we take the real wage as given. In that case, Sraffian economics concludes with the demonstration that it is possible to determine all relative prices in the economy and the rate of profit on capital simply from a specification of technology and an assumed wage-rate; consumer demand has nothing to do with it. Of course, demand determines *how much* of each product is produced but not at what *price* it will be sold; demand determines

[1] I have tried to explain Sraffian economics once before in an IEA publication: *The Cambridge Revolution: Success or Failure?* (London: IEA, Hobart Paperback No. 6, 2nd edn. 1975), pp. 21-32.

Figure 1

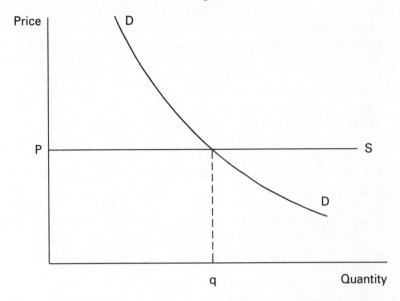

the *composition* of total output, and by implication the *volume* of total output, but not the relative *values* of one kind of output compared to another. We have returned to the labour theories of value of Adam Smith, David Ricardo and Karl Marx for whom prices were determined exclusively by the costs of production.

If we recall our elementary economics handed down since the days of Alfred Marshall a century ago, it appears that we are in a world where supply curves are horizontal lines, in consequence of which demand determines quantity but supply determines price (Figure 1). When supply curves are horizontal lines, it costs twice as much to produce a double amount of anything, three times as much to produce a triple amount, and so on; unit costs are constant because a large plant is simply a small plant scaled up. In the short run, this is an almost inconceivable case – you can always squeeze a bit more out of any plant even when it is operated at full capacity but only at rising costs per unit of output. But in the long run, that is, when all possible ways of producing more output have been exhausted, it is a perfectly conceivable case. It is the case which Marshall labelled 'constant returns to scale'.

[23]

Early in his career, when he was only 28 years old, Sraffa made his reputation with an article, 'The Laws of Returns under Competitive Conditions' (1926), in which he argued that, from a strictly logical point of view, the only long-run supply curve that properly represents the general run of cases in a perfectly competitive economy is, not a normal upward-sloping or a perverse downward-sloping supply curve, but a horizontal, constant-cost supply curve. Sraffa spent the rest of his life editing the works, speeches and letters of Ricardo. Then in 1960 he produced the mysterious little book[1] which demonstrated that the only admissible case of perfectly competitive price determination, the case of constant costs, is precisely the one which rules out factor substitution in response to changing factor prices, which is the be-all and end-all of marginalist economics. It implies that fixed-coefficients of production, or a 'linear technology' as we would say nowadays, form the appropriate general framework for thinking about price determination in the real world. It follows from this that demand is not co-ordinate with supply in determining prices, that consumers are not sovereign and indeed have no direct influence on the pricing process, and in particular that factor prices are not determined in the same way as the prices of consumer goods.

This explains why John Eatwell, in a key entry in The New Palgrave on Returns to Scale (IV: 165-6), is absolutely adamant in denying that there is any such thing as real-world decreasing or increasing returns to scale – unit costs falling or rising as plants get bigger. According to him, the famous long-run U-shaped cost curve of the standard textbooks (Figure 2) is a bogus concept and 'the only really satisfactory formal characterisation of returns of scale is that of constant returns' (IV: 166; also IV: 448). So, if he is to be believed, it is simply meaningless to talk about an *optimum* plant designed to minimise unit costs, which implies that plants can be too large or too small, and it is equally meaningless to define a 'natural monopoly' in the standard way as an industry whose technology dictates a scale of operations so large that average costs are minimised with only one monopoly

---

[1] P. Sraffa, *Production of Commodities by Means of Commodities* (London: Cambridge University Press, 1960).

Figure 2

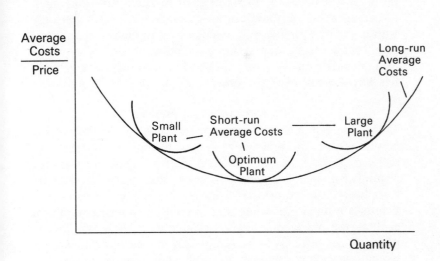

producer. In any case, the motive for Eatwell's assault on the standard orthodox doctrine of varying returns to scale is to defend the neglect of demand in Sraffa's theory of value.[1]

Sraffa had to assume the wage-rate to get any answers at all, and that wage-rate is therefore determined outside the model by political rather than economic factors, by the class struggle rather than the process of competition – fill in whatever you like. In Sraffian language, the theory of value is divorced from the theory of distribution and, moreover, the latter takes priority over the former. First we take a distributional variable as determined by political forces, and then with the aid of a set of engineering blueprints for the production of every commodity in the system we can solve for all relative prices in our economic model, including the remaining distributional variables. So, goodbye to

---

[1] The issue of varying returns to scale is not just an argument about the theory of the firm, because Nicholas Kaldor and Martin Weitzman have argued that some form of increasing returns to scale is a necessary condition for genuine involuntary unemployment *à la* Keynes. If there were strictly constant returns to scale in all aspects of technology, there could be no involuntary unemployment because any unemployed worker could always set himself up as a mini-firm (see S. Vassilakis on Increasing Return to Scale, II: 763).

the theory of consumer behaviour and the so-called marginal productivity theory of distribution of neo-classical economics, according to which trade unions can influence wages but only within definite limits, and goodbye in particular to general equilibrium theory, that strange, orthodox doctrine that everything depends on everything else and that no economic variable has any priority over any other. And all this in 92 pages!

'Beautiful Technical Puzzles'

This is the gist of Sraffa's central message but along the way his book, despite its brevity, generates a number of beautiful technical puzzles, most of which it then proceeds to solve. For example, it had long been known that 'joint production' complicates the exposition of almost any theory of value and defeats any theory of value that is entirely supply-determined, such as the old labour theory of value or Sraffa's own linear-production model. By 'joint production' we mean a situation in which two or more outputs are produced inseparably from the same set of inputs, the familiar examples being meat and wool from sheep and petrol and oil from petroleum. Such cases were traditionally regarded as somewhat exceptional but Sraffa, inspired by some older classical discussions of the issue, realised that they invariably arise in every use of fixed capital in the sense that production employing machinery typically produces some final product and, as a by-product, an older but still usable machine; in other words, every instance of production employing durable capital is an example of joint production.

Now in the first part of his book, Sraffa gets rid of the complication of joint production by examining only cases of single-product industries employing 'circulating capital', that is, raw materials and short-lived implements that are fully used up in one cycle of production. For this sort of make-believe world he generates a number of his elegant results, which, however, are not sustained for the real-world case of multi-product industries employing fixed capital examined in part two of his book. Since the book contains no conclusion, it is left to the reader to decide whether any of the elegant theorems of part one are of much practical significance. In any case, so many hints and allusions of how the apparatus might conceivably be amplified are strewn along the way that there is plenty of scope for the analytically

[26]

inclined disciple to refine and extend the model.[1] A veritable academic industry has grown up extolling and elaborating Sraffian economics. As Paul Samuelson asks in his highly critical account of Sraffian economics in The New Palgrave: 'Did any scholar have so great an impact on economic science as Piero Sraffa did in so few writings?' (IV: 460).[2]

Re-interpreting History

With Sraffa as the fountain-head of a new brand of non-marginalist economics, Ricardo and Marx appear naturally as predecessors and Keynes and Kalecki as fellow-travellers, similarly rejecting orthodox economics but from a macro-economic rather than a micro-economic standpoint. The result is a far-reaching Sraffian re-interpretation of the entire history of economic thought. The economic thinking of the last 200 years, Sraffians tell us, reveals two great branches: a general equilibrium branch leading down from Jevons, Walras and Marshall to the neo-classical economics of the Arrows and Samuelsons of today, in which all the relevant economic variables are mutually and simultaneously determined, and a Ricardo-Marx-Sraffa branch in which distribution takes priority over pricing because economic variables are causally determined in a sequential chain starting from a pre-determined real wage. This re-interpretation has been disseminated in a number of books and articles by Sraffian True Believers over the last 20 years and is given full-star billing in The New Palgrave. It figures prominently in Garegnani's 12,000-word essay on the Surplus Approach to Value and Distribution (IV: 560-73), whose basic elements, he insists, are to be found in what others previously labelled English classical political economy.

The notion that Sraffa's 1960 book is at once the revival and culmination of a grand old tradition that was first buried and then forgotten by those wicked neo-classical economists involves a great deal of making-it-up-as-you-go-along accounts

---

[1] For references to such refinements, Neri Salvadori on Basics and Non-Basics (I: 201).

[2] It is worth noting that this essay by Samuelson was unsolicited, as is made evident by the publisher's early Prospectus for The New Palgrave (August 1986) in which Samuelson is listed as writing on 'Wicksell and neo-classical economics' but not on 'Sraffian economics'.

of what such classical economists as Adam Smith, David Ricardo, John Stuart Mill and Karl Marx actually believed. They took as given, we are told, the available technology, the real wage-rate and both the volume and composition of total output, and on the basis of these parameters explained the determination of relative prices and the rate of profit or interest (Garegnani, IV: 560-2; Giorgio Gilibert, I: 424; C. A. Gregory, I: 613; Eatwell, I: 3, 538, 539, 698, III: 599; Heinz Kurz, I: 357; Massimo Pivetti, I: 872-5; Carlo Panico, II: 106, 877; Geoffrey Harcourt, III: 924). How extraordinary that this is precisely what Sraffa did! In other words, Adam Smith's *Inquiry into the Nature and Causes of the Wealth of Nations* is not, as many of us have believed, a study of the factors conducive to growth and development in a dynamic capitalist society but rather an essay in the theory of price determination in a stationary state *à la* Sraffa, according to which all variations in output are ruled out by definition. Similarly, Ricardo's *Principles of Political Economy and Taxation* is not a study of the natural resource scarcities that erode the inducement to invest in a tariff-ridden economy like that of Britain in the years after the Napoleonic Wars but a technical exercise in the distributional implications of 'the corn model', a primitive version of Sraffa's 'standard commodity' (G. De Vivo, I: 671, IV: 183-98; Donald Harris, I: 446).

First we read Sraffian economics backwards into the works of Smith, Ricardo and John Stuart Mill and then we proclaim with triumph: 'Sraffa (1960) deserves the credit for having elaborated a consistent formulation of the classical surplus approach to the problem of capital and distribution' (Heinz Kurz, I: 359).

But enough said. My essay on Classical Economics in The New Palgrave (especially I: 439-42) attempts to sort out the sense and nonsense in the surplus interpretation of English classical political economy and I shall not go over that ground again here. Interestingly enough, not a single one of the articles on the surplus approach to value and distribution in classical economics written by Sraffians and cited above contains any cross-reference to my own essay on classical economics.

All this is far from an antiquarian intellectual issue. Every new paradigm or school of thought in economics must sooner or later acquire its own pedigree because a new way of looking at the present always entails a new way of looking at the past. At the same time, a new way of looking at the past instils confidence in the belief that one has at long last found the one and only truth and can become a powerful method of enlisting new devotees. It is no wonder then that Sraffian economics has invaded the history of economic thought, seeking to supplant the standard neoclassical interpretations of what the economists of the past were all about.

III

MARXIAN ECONOMICS

MARXIAN ECONOMICS presents a special problem to Sraffians. In one sense, Marx was the last of the classical economists whose thinking was thoroughly steeped in the concepts and modes of thought of Ricardo. However, Marx was also highly critical of Ricardo for his failure to consider economic problems in an historical context, and the Marxian 'vision' soared above that of Ricardo and even the larger vision of Adam Smith and John Stuart Mill. Moreover, there is so much growth and development economics in Marx, so much economic dynamics focussed on technical progress and business cycles, that Marxian economics cannot be easily fitted into a history of economics which has Sraffa standing at its very pinnacle. Indeed, Sraffian economics has already produced its first great heresy. Ian Steedman's brilliant book on *Marx after Sraffa* (1977)[1] employs Sraffa's apparatus to argue that the labour theory of value in Marx is not only redundant but actually unworkable as soon as joint products and choice of techniques are admitted into the analysis. Orthodox Marxists reacted with fury to this neo-Ricardian apostasy (Steedman, 1981; Fine, 1986; also Murray Milgate on Neo-Ricardianism, II: 637).[2] And to this day Sraffian economics has a neo-Marxist and a post-Marxist wing, that is, those who

[1] London: New Left Books.
[2] I have discussed the Steedman critique of Marx in more detail elsewhere: in my *Methodological Appraisal of Marxian Economics* (Amsterdam: North-Holland Publishing, 1980), pp. 18-23.

TABLE 3: **Entries on Marxian Economics**

Author	Vol./Pages
Edualdo Da Silva	I: 4-5, IV: 749-51
Anwar Shaikh	I: 9-10, 333-6, II: 249-51, III: 347-8, 755-7, IV: 574-6
George Catephores	I: 76-8
A. Hussain	I: 495-6
Willi Semmler	I: 540-2
N. Okishio	I: 580-4
Andrew Glynn	I: 638-40, III: 390-4
Peter Kenway	I: 724-6, IV: 105-7
Alice Amsden	II: 728-33
G. De Vivo	III: 88-9
William Lazonick	III: 89-92
Ernst Mandel	III: 367-82
John Roemer	III: 383-6
Richard Jessop	III: 489-91
Paul Sweezy	III: 541-4
Ross Thomson	III: 963-6
Fabio Petri	IV: 66-8
Meghnad Desai	IV: 335-7, 789-91
E. K. Hunt	IV: 688-90
Krishna Bharadwaj	IV: 830-2

rank Sraffa below and those who, like Steedman, rank him above Marx.

None of these internecine battles is allowed to appear in The New Palgrave. Literally every article on Marxian economics in the four volumes is written by an avowed Marxist (Table 3). And although Steedman is a contributor to The New Palgrave he was not invited to give an account of his Sraffa-inspired critique of Marx. To say that the treatment of Marx in The New Palgrave is one-sided is to state the obvious. To give just one example, there is a perfectly appalling entry on the Labour theory of value by Fernando Viannello (III: 107-13), which concludes that the only thing that can be said against the labour theory of value is that it cannot be defended in the way that Marx defended it. This is rather like reading an entry on phlogiston in a dictionary of chemistry that calmly sets out the pros and cons of phlogiston theory and then chides Joseph Priestley for defending it poorly. How could the editors have passed an entry like this one?

IV

Keynesian Economics

An important part of the Sraffian history of economic thought is the Keynesian epoch and precisely why the Keynesian Revolution failed in the 1950s to be replaced first by 'the neo-classical synthesis' and, then, by monetarism in the 1960s and rational expectations in the 1970s. The standard reason given for the collapse of Keynesian economics is the appearance of 'stagflation' in the late 1960s and early 1970s and the apparent failure of Keynesian economics to explain the phenomenon. But a contributory reason was the lack of a coherent micro-foundation for the macro-economic hypotheses of Keynes. The Sraffian account of the demise of the Keynesian Revolution, however, is quite different. It is that Keynes' message was vulgarised and distorted; that its profoundly anti-orthodox implications were quietly buried and that Keynes himself sowed the seeds of that demise by compromising with the neo-classical theory of value and distribution. It follows that a consistent Keynesian must complete the revolution that Keynes inaugurated by repudiating neo-classical economics in its entirety.

This Sraffian story is set forth in a large number of entries in The New Palgrave on the Keynesian Revolution, and indeed in almost enough entries to neutralise Don Patinkin's long, brilliant biographical entry on Keynes, which runs for 22 pages along standard lines. The balanced tone of Patinkin's essay is thus offset by Murray Milgate's strident entry on Keynes' *General Theory* (III: 46-7). This is immediately followed by three tendentious pages on the Keynesian Revolution by Lorie Tarshis (III: 47-50), and elsewhere essays by Geoffrey Harcourt on Bastard Keynesianism (I: 203-4) and Post-Keynesian Economics

[31]

(IV: 924-7), Carlo Panico on Liquidity Preference (III: 213-6), and a programmatic statement by John Eatwell on Imperfectionist Models (II: 726-8) complete the Sraffian story of how the revolution in both vision and method which Keynes inaugurated was gradually but steadily betrayed by a veritable conspiracy on the part of those evil orthodox economists.

V

THE SWITCHING DEBATE

APART FROM believing that Sraffa has now provided them with a solid core of value and distribution theory upon which to build a new economics, Sraffians are also convinced that neo-classical economics contains a fatal logical flaw: capital cannot be valued independently of the rate of profit or interest and therefore the latter cannot be determined by the marginal productivity of capital as orthodox theory requires. Furthermore, a technique of production that is rendered unprofitable by a rise in the rate of interest may become once more profitable by a further rise in the rate of interest, a paradoxical result known as 'reswitching'. Finally, in consequence of reswitching, we cannot in general draw a negatively inclined demand curve for capital – we cannot in general argue that a fall in the rate of interest will induce more investment, and vice versa for a rise in the rate of interest. Having at one time denied all this, the leaders of neo-classical economics now concede the possibility of both reswitching and 'capital-reversing' (Tatsuo Hatta, I: 354-6; and Samuelson, IV: 437; see also Heinz Kurz, I: 347-62; Luigi Pasinetti and Roberto Scazzieri, I: 363-7, IV: 162-4, 172-3).[1] But, of course, they deny that it implies the demise of neo-classical economics; what it implies, they say, is the falseness of some simple parables of orthodox classroom teaching, as for example that economic growth requires more 'waiting' because roundabout production is time-consuming, which extra waiting will always depress the rate of

---

[1] Tatsuo Hatta argues that reswitching and capital-reversing is 'Fully explicable within neo-classical theory, being no more (and no less) than one of the many intractable problems caused by the presence of complementarity' (I: 356).

[32]

interest, which will invariably stimulate additional investment, and so on and on.

Exceptions Prove the Rule!

The Sraffian conviction that neo-classical economics is fatally defective because it does not permit invariant generalisations about the relationship between the relevant economic variables must stem from the prior belief that there are universal 'laws' of economics. Only when there are universal laws can we say that exceptions disprove the rule. But there are no *universal* laws of economics. As every Cambridge student of elementary economics knows, even the famous 'law of demand' that price is inversely related to quantity has an exception in the case of Giffen goods, the demand for which *increases* if their price is raised. Nevertheless, we do not for that reason abandon the presumption that demand curves are highly likely to be negatively inclined if only because no statistician has ever produced a convincing example of a positively inclined demand curve (Donald Walker on Giffen Goods, II: 523-4; also III: 798). Similarly, we can easily prove that supply curves may be negatively inclined, so that a rise in price induces a *reduction* in supply, and yet we continue to insist that they are positively inclined in the overwhelming preponderance of cases, a rise in price inducing an increase in supply. In short, we make use of the Marshallian cross of demand and supply in almost every piece of economic reasoning but we know perfectly well that our general rules have exceptions. We simply say with Marshall that 'the central doctrines of Economics are not simple and cannot be made so'. Why should we not adopt a similar attitude to reswitching and capital-reversing? It is true that they are *possible* but it is also true that they are highly *unlikely*, and that as yet no one has observed a single real-world example of either reswitching or capital-reversing – as Edmond Malinvaud points out (II: 960).

It is ironic that the intolerance of Sraffians to any exception whatsoever to the standard neo-classical theorems is matched by a great deal of tolerance towards complications introduced into Sraffa's model by the presence of joint production. Thus, in the second part of Sraffa's *Production of Commodities by Means of Commodities*, dealing with multi-product industries and the use of fixed capital as a leading species of the genus of joint products,

[33]

Sraffa notes that his 'standard commodity' may now include negative amounts of some commodities, that the relative value of commodities can no longer be reduced to 'dated quantities of labour', and that one cannot even be certain that the real wage is always inversely related to the rate of profit: in short, that the famous Sraffian yardstick, the standard commodity, and the equally acclaimed linear wage-profit frontier of single-product industries probably has no economic significance in a real world of multi-product industries (John Woods on Invariable Standard of Value, II: 969, and Bertram Schefold on Joint Production, II: 1,031-2). This is not in itself a reason for discarding the whole of Sraffa, but it is certainly to say that there are no universal truths in Sraffa just as there are none in Walras and Marshall.

Mid-air Economics

The house that Sraffa built is an elegant construction, full of wonderful and surprising nooks and crannies, but it has its foundations planted firmly in mid-air. The degree of abstraction adopted by Sraffa is so high that even questions of economies or diseconomies of scale cannot arise because changes in the absolute amount of any input or output are rigorously excluded. Thus, we may not ask whether supply curves are negatively or positively inclined because there are no supply *curves* in Sraffa: producers do not supply more or less at various prices for the simple reason that prices never vary; they simply are what they are in consequence of assumed technology and a certain rate of wages for labour. Taking certain data as lying outside the realm of an economic model developed for one purpose does not of course preclude a theoretical explanation of their determination at a later stage for another purpose. Sraffa's book was published in 1960, and one might have expected that some progress would have been made in the intervening 28 years in the analysis of the size and composition of output, choice of techniques – if there is indeed a choice – and the real wage of a capitalist economy. But as a matter of fact, Sraffian economics has been almost wholly moribund. Even Sraffa's prolegomenon to a critique of orthodox economics has never been extended or refined.[1] Some of the brain-teasers that Sraffa introduced, such as reswitching and

[1] The one promising extension has been that of Steedman and Metcalfe to the Heckscher-Ohlin-Samuelson theory of international trade (Steedman, 1979).

joint production, have indeed been further explored but not a single application of the Sraffian model to the 'way things are' has been forthcoming in 28 years. Yes, it takes a long time in economics to make any practical use of theoretical innovations but, surely, it is time to ask whether it is perhaps something about the very nature of Sraffa's approach that has so far made it totally irrelevant to practical issues.

VI

GENERAL EQUILIBRIUM THEORY

THERE IS a trade-off in economics between rigour and relevance. Theories that are truly rigorous are rarely practically relevant, and theories that are eminently relevant to practical questions are rarely rigorous analytically. We witness this trade-off in Sraffian economics and we witness it again in general equilibrium theory, that jewel in the crown of neo-classical economics.

Proof not Practice

There is, moreover, an intimate connection between Sraffian economics and general equilibrium theory. Frank Hahn (1984, p. 353) has said quite rightly that 'there is no correct neo-Ricardian proposition which is not contained in the set of propositions which can be generated by orthodoxy'; and by 'orthodoxy' he means a disaggregated general equilibrium theory as found in the writings of, say, Arrow and Debreu. General equilibrium theory was invented more than a century ago by Leon Walras who was the first to seize on multi-market equilibria as the central economic problem, and to pose its solution as analogous to the algebraic problem of solving a set of simultaneous equations. Walras' procedure was to write down a set of abstract demand and supply equations on the assumption of perfect competition, perfect price flexibility and perfect factor mobility and then to 'prove' the existence of a solution for this set of simultaneous equations by counting the number of equations and unknowns; if they were equal, he concluded that simultaneous equilibrium in all markets was at least possible.

This strictly static picture of the determination of equilibrium was then followed up by a quasi-realistic explanation of how the competitive mechanism might establish such an equilibrium in practice, namely by automatic price adjustments in response to the appearance of excess demand and supply. Walras labelled these adjustments 'tâtonnement', that is, 'groping' by trial and error on the part of independently acting buyers and sellers, and their role in general equilibrium theory troubled him all his life.

The task which he had set himself was to show that the relative prices which emerge from the process of competition are the same as the roots of his system of demand and supply equations in which the unknowns are the equilibrium quantities and prices. The difficulty was to allow for disequilibrium trading at other than market-clearing prices because these alter the distribution of goods among buyers and sellers before equilibrium is reached, thus changing the final equilibrium solution itself to one that differs from that dictated by the original set of equations. Walras hankered initially after a realistic description of the temporal sequence of price adjustments by which actual markets reach a final equilibrium solution. Indeed, he was persuaded by studies of the Paris stock exchange that his own mechanism of tâtonnement, in which prices are altered by a fictional auctioneer in accordance with excess demand or supply but no quantities are allowed to be exchanged until the equilibrium price is reached, might be construed as an example drawn from real life. But in successive formulations of his theory, he gradually abandoned the aim of descriptive realism and settled for the view that the tâtonnement process was at best an abstract model of how real-world markets move to equilibrium.

Competition as Outcome Rather than Process

Markets for most goods and services are not like auctions at Christie's or Sotheby's, and in this sense we can conclude only that Walras ultimately gave up the effort to provide a convincing account of how real-world competitive markets achieve multi-market equilibrium. In some sense such an account has never been provided even to this day. Of course, modern mathematical economists establish the existence, stability and determinacy of general equilibrium by more elegant reasoning than that employed by Walras – for example, they introduce the unrealistic but highly simplifying assumption that there are forward markets for absolutely all goods and services in the economy – but that is not to be confused with a realistic description of actual buying and selling, involving costly acquisition of information about alternative trading opportunities and the irreversible lapses of time between successive transactions.

Modern Austrian economists, such as Friedrich Hayek, Israel Kirzner and Don Lavoie, go so far as to suggest that the Walrasian approach to the problem of general equilibrium is a *cul de sac*: if we want to understand the *process* of competition rather than the nature of the end-state achieved by competition, we must begin by discarding such *static* reasoning as is implied by any and all versions of general equilibrium. And, indeed, it is a shocking truth that modern economics comes equipped with a rich analysis of the nature of equilibrium as the final outcome of the workings of the competitive mechanism and yet is virtually silent on the precise means by which buyers and sellers resolve their differences on the way to final equilibrium. It is as if a cartographer supplied us with a detailed map of Rome, assured us that all roads led to it, and yet could give us no indication of how one actually sets about going to Rome. This failure to give an account of the process of competition is shocking because most of the acclaimed virtues of competition derive from its dynamic characteristics in fostering technical dynamism and cost-cutting innovations. But these are the disequilibrium features of the process of competition that have disappeared by the time we come to consider the final equilibrium. In short, whatever the virtues of equilibrium analysis, it is of little help in explaining the true merits of competition.

Abstraction or Description?

It is interesting to note that attitudes to Walrasian general equilibrium theory have gone through a 180-degree revolution since Walras' own times. Walras himself seems to have conceived of his model as an admittedly abstract but not misleading representation of the manner in which competition drives prices to their equilibrium values in a capitalist régime. Similarly, when general equilibrium theory was revived in the 1930s, having almost disappeared from view in the previous 50 years, it was common to regard it as a reasonable approximation to the description of an actual capitalist economy. Thus, in the great Socialist Calculation Debate of the 1930s, Oskar Lange argued that socialism could employ a procedure for equilibrating prices that was similar to that ostensibly employed under capitalism, namely a Walrasian *tâtonnement* (Tadeusz Kowalik on the Lange-Lerner Mechanism, III: 129-31, and W. Brus on Market Socialism, III: 337).[1] However, the Walrasian system is nowadays defended as a purely formal statement of the concept of general equilibrium, telling us what we *mean* by a logically consistent equilibrium model; not even the most enthusiastic advocates of general equilibrium theory pretend for one moment that it provides any kind of description of or prescription for a capitalist economy.

Since general equilibrium theory is no longer regarded as having much, if any, empirical content, it might be advisable to discard the very term 'general equilibrium *theory*' and to speak instead of general equilibrium as a 'framework' or 'paradigm'. This indeed accords with the practice of its most prominent spokesmen (Hahn, 1984, pp. 45-6). Enormous intellectual resources have been invested in the last 40-50 years in continually refining and elaborating this general equilibrium framework. Yet it is questionable even now whether these efforts have thrown any light on the way economic systems function in practice. Worse than that is the thought that the general equilibrium construction, by its very nature of emphasising the end-state rather than the process of competition, may be the wrong starting point from which to approach a substantive explanation of the workings of an economic system.

[1] Despite subject entries on socialism, socialist economics and market socialism, and biographical entries on Oskar Lange and Ludwig von Mises, the Socialist Calculation Debate, so crucial to the revival of general equilibrium theory and the rise of modern welfare economics in the 1930s, is nowhere discussed at length in The New Palgrave (Lavoie, 1985).

VII

BACK TO SRAFFA

BUT WHAT has all this to do with Sraffian economics? Simply this: Sraffian economics, like Walrasian economics, is obsessed with the mathematical metaphor of simultaneous equations, with the counting of equations and unknowns, with the end-state equilibrium solution of a set of relative prices rather than the process of prices groping towards their equilibrium values. How do we know in Sraffa that the real wage is a datum that is not determined by the same economic forces that govern all other prices? Because there are not enough equations to determine all relative prices as well as the rate of profit and the rate of wages. The *form* of the argument is exactly the same as that of Walras; the *content* is different only because Sraffa makes different assumptions from those employed by Walras.[1] Sraffians like to claim that distributional variables are determined prior to the prices of final goods and services, but their theory baldly asserts this by assumption – it does not establish this, or indeed any other, *causal* claim about the sequential determination of economic variables.

Sraffa, like Walras, believed that a satisfactory theory of value and distribution in a capitalist economy should explain the long-period position of the economy. Long-period analysis has been largely abandoned in mainstream economics since about the 1920s, to be replaced by short-period analysis of temporary equilibria. This is something which Sraffians regard as one of the most deplorable features of modern orthodox economics, and they hope to bring about a renaissance of the economics of the long run (Carlo Panico and Fabio Petri on Long-run and Short-run, III: 238-40, and Eatwell on Natural and Normal Conditions, III: 598-9). But this slavish commitment to long-period analysis merely exacerbates the practical irrelevance of most Sraffian economics. Keynes once contemptuously dismissed the long run as a situation in which we are all dead:

'Economists set themselves too easy, too useless a task if in

---

[1] In an entry on Models and Theory, Vivian Walsh struggles unconvincingly to deny this assertion (III: 483).

tempestuous seasons they can only tell us that when the storm is long past the ocean is flat again'.[1]

Yet this is precisely that which Sraffians seek to make the only world that economics must address.

Theory Without Relevance

The empirical content of both Sraffian and Walrasian economics is nil because no theoretical system couched in such completely general terms could possibly predict any economic event or, to use Popperian language, forbid any economic event that might conceivably occur. It is true that Walrasian systems can be simplified by aggregation, as for example the famous Hicks-Hansen IS-LM version of Keynesian economics reduced to four equations; it is also true that the qualitative or comparative static properties of such simplified general equilibrium systems can be checked against empirical observations (does investment increase when the interest rate declines?, and so forth). Likewise, Herbert Scarf's computational algorithm for solving general equilibrium systems (I: 556-62) has encouraged a number of economists in recent years to employ large-scale general equilibrium models to provide numerical estimates of the impact of policy changes, such as amendments of the tax system. But few of these models have been tested to check whether they give more accurate answers than much simpler partial equilibrium models (T. J. Kehoe on Comparative Statics, I: 517-21). And let us not forget that the superiority of such applied general equilibrium models is fundamentally an empirical question because their construction is costly. Taking account of all interdependencies is in some sense better than ignoring them, but it is also much harder work and the pay-off in predictability may not warrant the extra effort. In any case, the construction of *applied* general equilibrium models is a far cry from abstract proofs of the existence, stability and determinacy of *theoretical* general equilibrium models, which have earned several economists the kudos of a Nobel prize.

As for theoretical general equilibrium models, it is worth noting that all-round multi-market equilibrium is a feature of certain *models* of the economy and not necessarily a reflection of

[1] J. M. Keynes (1971), p. 65.

how that economy is constituted. Counting the number of linear equations and unknowns to make sure that they are equal is a necessary condition for the existence of a mathematical solution of a set of simultaneous equations, which is *analogous* to the simultaneous determination of a set of equilibrium prices in all the markets of an economy, but that is not to say that prices are actually determined simultaneously; a *sequential* process of price determination – first the price of coal, then the price of steel, and then the price of automobiles – is perhaps a more plausible representation of how prices come to be set in the course of competitive rivalry.

In any case, the question is not one of approving or condemning the Walrasian apparatus in toto but of deciding whether it deserves quite as high a place in the pecking order of professional prestige in economics as it currently enjoys; in particular, whether it does not constitute something like a blind alley, an intellectual game, from the standpoint of generating substantive hypotheses about economic behaviour. As Franklin Fisher puts it in his brief but illuminating entry on Adjustment Processes and Stability:

'the very power and elegance of [general] equilibrium analysis often obscures the fact that it rests on a very uncertain foundation. We have no similarly elegant theory of what happens *out* of equilibrium, of how agents behave when their plans are frustrated. As a result, we have no rigorous basis for believing that equilibrium can be achieved or maintained if disturbed' (I: 26; also John Geanakoplos, I: 123).

This lacuna in general equilibrium theory produces the curious anomaly that perfect competition is possible only when a market is in equilibrium. It is impossible when a market is out of equilibrium for the simple reason that perfectly competitive producers are price-takers, not price-makers. But if no-one can make the price, how do prices ever change to produce convergence on equilibrium? (Jean-Paul Benassy on Disequilibrium Analysis, I: 858-62; also A. P. Kirman on Measure Theory, III: 434-5). But, despite such admissions of the severe limitations of the Walrasian apparatus (see also Paul McNulty on Competition, Austrian Conception, I: 536-7, and Thomas Rothenberg on Simultaneous Equations Models, IV: 344-7), most of those writing on general equilibrium theory in The New Palgrave have little doubt of its usefulness (Frank Hahn, I: 136-8; Herbert Scarf, I: 556; Gerard Debreu, II: 216-8, III: 402; Lionel McKenzie, II: 509-10; and Takashi Negishi, IV: 595). Unfortunately, they never specify the criteria by which they judge its positive utility.[1]

VIII

METHODOLOGY

THE EDITORS of The New Palgrave were no doubt disinclined to question any claims of practical relevance on behalf of general equilibrium theory if only because 'what is sauce for the goose . . .'. After all, the peculiarity of the Sraffian critique of orthodox economics is that Sraffian economics is itself a species of the genus of general equilibrium models and has to be defended, in formal terms, in the same way that general equilibrium theory is defended. Those who lay siege to a citadel defended by gunpowder cannot afford to renounce the use of explosives!

Thus, Sraffians have a vested interest in the methodological faith that patently abstract economic theories may somehow contain startling implications for economic policy. How this trick is performed is never explained and in general The New Palgrave gives little guidance on the crucial issue of the connection between theory and policy. Mainstream economists are frequently too sanguine about the practical relevance of abstract economic theory, but at least they pay lip-service to the doctrine that economic theories, like all scientific theories, must ultimately be judged in terms of their testable implications for economic events. Sraffian economists, on the other hand, deny this methodological standard which indeed they are fond of ascribing to the noxious influence of the philosophy of 'positivism' on modern economics (Shaun Hargreaves-Heap and Martin Hollis on Determinism, I: 876-8). No wonder then that virtually all the entries on methodology in The New Palgrave are devoted to denouncing empirical evidence as the litmus paper test of substantive propositions in economics (for

[1] J. Geanakoplos in a penetrating essay on the Arrow-Debreu model of general equilibrium (I: 16-24) expresses a number of doubts about it but he too fails to reveal his standards.

[42]

example, Hargreaves-Heap on Epistemological Issues in Economics, II: 166-8).[1] In that light, the absence of entries for Testing, Falsification, Verification and Validation in The New Palgrave takes on a new meaning.

Limitations of Econometric Methods

Stefano Zamagni tells us quite rightly that

> 'since no scientific law, in the natural scientific sense, has been established in economics, on which economists can base predictions, what are used and have to be used to explain or to predict are tendencies or patterns expressed in empirical or historical generalisations of less than universal validity, restricted by local and temporal limits' (II: 54).

But N. F. R. Crafts, in a perceptive discussion of the contribution of economics to economic history, concedes that 'most work applying economics to history does not involve tests of competing hypotheses', and that the 'new economic history', which does involve such tests, employs standards of proof that are too low to convince the sceptical historian (II:39). That leaves us with econometrics as a method of testing 'tendencies or patterns' expressed in empirical generalisations. There was a time, just before and after World War II, when great hopes were pinned on econometrics as the means by which economic theories might be conclusively appraised. But in recent years a deep sense of malaise has come over the subject as the severe limitations of econometric methods have come home to its practitioners. Economic theories abound in unobservable latent variables, poorly specified *ceteris paribus* clauses, and unspecified functional forms and dynamic relationships. These theories are then tested on data that are the legal by-products of public and private economic transactions rather than the results of specially designed experiments. No wonder then that econometric results are almost always ambiguous.[2]

[1] Lawrence Boland, no Sraffian, writes an entry on Methodology (III: 455-8) but hardly mentions testing, falsification and verification. Similarly, he writes on Stylised Facts (IV: 535-6) in Kaldorian growth theory but ignores the *fact* that almost all of Kaldor's stylised facts were not facts at all (H. Uzawa on Models of Growth, III: 485).

[2] Stanley Fisher reports that Samuelson's 'major disappointment in economics in the last forty years has been the failure of econometric evidence to settle disputes' (IV: 240).

Nevertheless I would agree with Hashem Pesaran's pessimistic survey of econometric accomplishments, which concludes that the only cure for the shortcomings of econometrics is more and better econometrics (II: 19). The central issue remains that of choosing among competing economic theories in the light of empirical evidence, that is, to provide some external check on our wish to believe what we would like to believe. That issue is barely touched upon in a rambling essay by Vivian Walsh on Philosophy and Economics (III: 861-8). Likewise, Bruce Caldwell tells us that Positivism is dead; but he has nothing to say on what might replace it (IV: 921-3). One answer to the death of positivism is rhetoric: the study and practice of persuasive expression. There are no methodological criteria for validating economic theories, Donald McCloskey tells us, but simply different reasons for believing them:

> 'Consider, for example, the sentence in economics, "The demand curve slopes down". The official rhetoric says that economists believe this because of statistical evidence – negative coefficients in demand curves for pig iron or negative diagonal items in matrices of complete systems of demand – accumulating steadily in journal articles. These are the tests 'consistent with the hypothesis'. Yet most beliefs in the hypothesis come from other sources: from introspection (what would I do?); from thought experiments (what would they do?); from uncontrolled cases in point (such as the oil crisis); from authority (Alfred Marshall believed it); from symmetry (a law of demand if there is a law of supply); from definition (a higher price leaves less for expenditure, including this one); and, above all, from analogy (if the demand curve slopes down for chewing gum, why not for housing and love too?). As may be seen in the classroom and seminar, the range of argument in economics is wider than the official rhetoric allows' (IV: 174).

But is the official rhetoric any better than the unofficial ones? Are there good reasons for believing any economic proposition and who is to tell us how to distinguish these from bad reasons? It used to be thought that the standards for appraising scientific theories came from a subject called 'philosophy of science' or 'methodology', but McCloskey would have us go even further than those who pronounce and welcome the death of positivism by pronouncing the death of anything called methodology.

[44]

McCloskey speaks idly of good and bad reasons for believing one or another economic theory but will not tell us how he knows whether a reason is good or bad.

But no matter.[1] The point is that McCloskey's 'rhetoric of economics' does at least aim to make economists acutely aware of their reasons for believing what they believe. One of my principal complaints of the endless reiteration of neo-Ricardian, Sraffian economics in The New Palgrave is that no reasons whatever are given for believing that Sraffian economics is better than any other economics. It is as if Sraffians believed that economic theories are embedded in self-contained and basically incommensurable 'paradigms', in consequence of which there can be no rational method of comparing the relative merits of different economic theories (Peter Urbach on Paradigms, III: 795-7). At any rate, I can see no other grounds for a simply astonishing failure to defend their firm belief in Sraffian economics by anything other than the bland declaration that it *is* significant.

IX

MORE METHODOLOGY

ECONOMICS IS a peculiar subject. It looks just like a science both in its formal structure and in its basic concern with observable reality. And yet economics does not reveal the sort of cumulative progress in the practical manipulation of reality that is one of the abiding characteristics of physics, chemistry, geology and parts of biology. Modern economists cannot predict either individual or aggregate economic behaviour very much better than Leon Walras could, or Adam Smith for that matter, and yet they remain committed to 'piecemeal social engineering', that is, to the use of collective action to improve the performance of the economy. It is not this that constitutes the peculiarity of economics as a subject because it may well be that the economy is simply harder to understand than Mother Nature, being less amenable to replicable laboratory experiments. The peculiarity

---

[1] I have examined McCloskey's *Rhetoric of Economics* (Madison: University of Wisconsin Press, 1986) elsewhere: 'Methodology with a small *m*', *Critical Review*, Vol. 1(2), Spring 1987.

of economics is rather that the vast majority of economists, whether orthodox or heterodox, are indifferent to the failure of economics to generate an ever-growing body of practically useful predictions on a par with the so-called 'hard' sciences.

Some economists even go so far as to say that economics is a kind of social mathematics that must be assessed in the same terms that we assess progress in pure mathematics. But even those who proclaim this view of economics – mathematical economists are naturally very fond of this sort of defence – admit that economics must take a stand on questions of economic policy and, of course, this implies that economists have knowledge of how the economic system functions: we *can* say whether privatisation improves the quantity and quality of the goods privatised; we *do* know whether exchange rates can be controlled and we also know whether this serves to control inflation; a reduction in the public sector borrowing requirement will cut down both inflation and unemployment; and so on. In other words, economics must be an empirical science, at least in part, in which case why is there so little concern with the poor empirical track-record of modern economics?

Ah, but all this is 'methodology' and methodology, any economist will tell you, is a dirty word, a subject peddled by people who like to talk about economics instead of doing it. The New Palgrave perfectly reflects this methodophobia of modern economics by the scant attention given to methodological topics, not to mention the persistent sneering at questions of empirical testing.

X

CONCLUSION

DESPITE DOZENS and perhaps as many as one hundred articles in The New Palgrave that I would not hesitate to recommend to anyone, I shudder to think that the work as a whole will have no rival for many decades to come and will probably remain the standard reference work on economics well into the next century.

It gives a hopelessly distorted picture of where economics is now. For better or for worse, and despite all the arguments and counter-arguments, the vast majority of economists the world over subscribe to the received corpus of neo-classical economics centred around the concepts of utility-maximising households and profit-maximising enterprises. There are Marxian economists, Radical economists, post-Keynesian economists, Behavioural economists, Experimental economists, old American Institutional economists, new Institutional economists, Evolutionary economists, and Austrian economists, but even all these added together only amount to a 25 per cent dissenting penumbra around a 75 per cent core of orthodoxy. On Mondays, Wednesdays and Fridays, I think that this is a good thing: economics is a solidly established profession with a definite point of view. On Tuesdays, Thursdays and Saturdays I deplore it: the orthodox majority stifles discussion and refuses to answer criticisms of its methods. But the fact remains that there is a broad consensus on a kind of economics which is consistently denigrated in every third or fourth entry of The New Palgrave.

Macmillan, the publisher of The New Palgrave, collected tributes to the volume prior to publication. Frank Hahn, Professor of Economics at Cambridge and current President of the Royal Economic Society, contributed the following encomium on the basis of what I take to be a selected sample of entries:

> 'For the doubtful the first move is to look for omitted topics. This will end in failure. The second move is to think of eminent economists who have not contributed. This too will fail. The third move will be to sample those entries on matters well known to the doubter. Here he will look for obscurities, slovenliness and incompleteness. He will largely look in vain. After that he is ready to learn and to enjoy himself. The Dictionary shows economics to be a discipline with exacting standards and considerable achievements ... one can now with confidence say to the critic: "go and consult Palgrave".'

I am one of the doubtful. I found it easy to tot up many omitted topics and even easier to think of eminent names that do not appear.[1] I also found many obscurities and instances of

[1] The list of contributors reads like a 'who's who' in economics, but not quite. I ought to know: a comparison of the names of the 900 contributors to The New Palgrave and the 1,000 most frequently cited living economists in my *Who's Who in Economics* (Brighton: Wheatsheaf Books, 2nd edn., 1986) shows an overlap of only about 500 names. Of course, those who do not appear in The New Palgrave may have been among the 200 or so economists who were asked to contribute but declined to do so (see I: x).

slovenliness and incompleteness. In addition, I repeatedly encountered examples of bias, special pleading and formalism.

I would rarely direct a *student* to any article in The New Palgrave but I might direct a *colleague* to consult it, drawing his attention, however, to the fact that it is at least in large part an encyclopedia of economics from a most peculiar and singular standpoint, namely, that of a small band of enthusiasts in Cambridge and various universities in Italy who seek to emulate the Keynesian Revolution by promoting a new brand of subversive economics that is Sraffian in theory and Marxian in politics. Orthodox economics, they contend, is little more than intellectual window-dressing for the political belief in the market as a self-regulating mechanism. To criticise orthodoxy is not enough because intellectuals abhor a mental vacuum as nature abhors a physical one. But Sraffa, Marx and Keynes somehow combined together to provide an alternative theoretical platform from which to launch the Holy War against neo-classical economics. From that perspective The New Palgrave is simply another fusillade in a continuous battle. The editors are, of course, entitled to their point of view but, when one considers that a dictionary of this kind only appears every 20-30 years and stands as a testimony to an entire generation of professional economists, one can only tear one's hair out at the magnitude of the opportunity that has been missed.

Bibliographical References

Colander, D. C., Klamer, A. (1987): 'The Making of an Economist', *Journal of Economic Perspectives*, I(2), Fall.

Fine, B. (ed.) (1986): *The Value Dimension. Marx Versus Ricardo and Sraffa*, London: Routledge & Kegan Paul.

Hahn, F. (1984): *Equilibrium and Macroeconomics*, Oxford: Blackwell.

Keynes, J. M. (1971): *A Tract on Monetary Reform*, in *The Collected Writings of John Maynard Keynes*, Vol. IV, London: Macmillan for the Royal Economic Society.

Lavoie, D. (1985): *Rivalry and Central Planning. The Socialist Calculation Debate Reconsidered*, Cambridge: Cambridge University Press.

Steedman, I. (1979): *Fundamental Issues in Trade Theory*, London: Macmillan.

Steedman, I., *et al.* (1981): *The Value Controversy*, London: New Left Books.

Some Recent IEA Papers

SOME PRESS COMMENTS ON
MARK BLAUG'S PREVIOUS IEA PAPER

The Cambridge Revolution: Success or Failure?

1975 Revised 2nd Edn.   Hobart Paperback No. 6   xiii + 102pp   £1·50

'... *The Cambridge Revolution: Success or Failure?* will make my reading lists.

The book covers seven topics in as many chapters (the aggregate production function, the Sraffa 'revolution', the reswitching issue, neo-classical income distribution, Cambridge theories of distribution, and the nature of profits), while the concluding eighth chapter contains Blaug's summary and judgement.'

EDWIN BURMEISTER, University of Pennsylvania,
Economic Record (Journal of The Economic Society of
Australia and New Zealand)

'... the book is a marvellous success as a polemic against the British Cambridge school, dissecting its deficiencies with the acute and penetrating logic of a master theoretician. In so doing it makes some important contributions to the debate as a whole, clarifies some of the issues, and takes the resolution of the problems several steps forward. Every economist interested in the fundamental logic of his subject should read it.'

DANIEL R. FUSFELD, University of Michigan,
History of Political Economy

'Professor Blaug has written a lively and interesting polemic and it should be promoted as such.'

BARBARA MACLENNAN
Department of Economics, University of Manchester,
The Times Higher Education Supplement

'... it is a ... professional work of scholarship in the history of thought and understanding of economic-theoretical method, which should be required reading for any student forced to read or academic scholar motivated to contribute to the usually arid and arcane technical literature on the reswitching controversy and the theoretical possibility of measuring the aggregate stock of capital.

Blaug begins with a clear literary exposition of the problems en-countered in the concept of an aggregate production function ... He then discusses the so-called Sraffa Revolution, more accurately described by Blaug as the "Rip-van-Winkle phenomenon".'

HARRY G. JOHNSON, University of Chicago,
Journal of Political Economy

IEA OCCASIONAL PAPERS in print

20. *The Confusion of Language in Political Thought* F. A. HAYEK. 1968 (2nd impression, 1976, £1.00)
23. *Politics and Economic Growth* GRAHAM HUTTON. 1968 (£1.00)
30. *Keynes and the Classics* AXEL LEIJONHUFVUD. 1969 (7th imp., 1981, £1.00)
*33. *The Counter-Revolution in Monetary Theory* MILTON FRIEDMAN. 1970 (5th imp., 1983, £1.00)
*35. *Wages and Prices in a Mixed Economy* JAMES E. MEADE. 1971 (£1.00)
36. *The Polluters: Industry or Government?* NEIL H. JACOBY & F. G. PENNANCE. 1972 (£1.00)
38. *Trade Unions: A Century of Privilege?* C. G. HANSON. 1973 (£1.00)
*39. *Economic Freedom and Representative Government* F. A. HAYEK. 1973 (3rd imp., 1980, £1.00)
40. *Lessons of Maplin* CHRISTOPHER FOSTER, J. B. HEATH, G. H. PETERS, J. E. FFOWCS WILLIAMS, SIR PETER MASEFIELD. 1974 (£1.00)
41. *Monetary Correction* MILTON FRIEDMAN. 1974 (3rd imp., 1978, £1.00)
44. *Unemployment versus Inflation?: An Evaluation of the Phillips Curve* MILTON FRIEDMAN, with a British Commentary by DAVID LAIDLER. 1975 (4th imp., 1981, £1.00)
45. *Full Employment at Any Price?* F. A. HAYEK. 1975 (The 1974 Alfred Nobel Memorial Lecture, 4th imp., 1978, £1.00)
*46. *Employment, Inflation and Politics* PETER JAY. 1976 (2nd imp., 1977, £1.00)
47. *Catch '76 . . .?* JOHN FLEMMING *et al.* 1976 (£1.50)
48. *Choice in Currency* F. A. HAYEK. 1976 (2nd imp., 1977, £1.00)
49. *From Galbraith to Economic Freedom* MILTON FRIEDMAN. 1977 (3rd imp., 1978, £1.00)
51. *Inflation and Unemployment: The New Dimension of Politics* (The 1976 Alfred Nobel Memorial Lecture) MILTON FRIEDMAN. 1977 (2nd imp., 1978, £1.00)
53. *Democracy and the Value of Money* WILLIAM REES-MOGG. 1977 (£1.00)
*54. *Economists and the British Economy* ALAN WALTERS. 1978 (£1.00)
*55. *Choice in European Monetary Union* ROLAND VAUBEL. 1979 (£1.00)
*56. *Whatever Happened to Productivity?* GRAHAM HUTTON. 1980 (£1.00)
58. *The End of Government . . .?* RALPH HARRIS. 1980 (£1.50)
*59. *What is Wrong with the European Communities?* J. B. DONGES. 1981 (£1.00)
60. *Wither the Welfare State* ARTHUR SELDON. 1981 (£1.50)
*61. *The Disorder in World Money: From Bretton Woods to SDRs* PAUL BAREAU. 1981 (£1.00)
62. *Could Do Better* MICHAEL BEENSTOCK, JO GRIMOND, RICHARD LAYARD, G. W. MAYNARD, PATRICK MINFORD, E. VICTOR MORGAN, M. H. PESTON, HAROLD ROSE, RICHARD C. STAPLETON, THOMAS WILSON, GEOFFREY WOOD. 1982 (£2.80)
63. *The Welfare State: For Rich or for Poor?* DAVID G. GREEN. 1982 (£1.20)
*64. *The Pleasures and Pains of Modern Capitalism* G. J. STIGLER. 1982 (£1.00)
65. *How Much Freedom for Universities?* H. S. FERNS, with an Economic Commentary by JOHN BURTON. 1982 (£1.50)
*66. *Myth and Reality in Anti-Trust* ARTHUR SHENFIELD. 1983 (£1.00)
67. *Who Cares?* ROBERT SUGDEN. 1983 (£1.50)
68. *Shoppers' Choice* RALPH HARRIS and ARTHUR SELDON. 1984 (£1.20)
69. *Pricing, Planning and Politics* SUBROTO ROY. 1984 (£1.80)
*70. *Economic Policy as a Constitutional Problem* JAN TUMLIR. 1984 (£1.00)
71. *No, Minister!* RALPH HARRIS. 1985 (£1.80)
72. *Wage-Fixing Revisited* J. E. MEADE. 1985 (£1.50)
*73. *Two Cheers for Self-Interest:* Some Moral Prerequisites of a Market Economy SAMUEL BRITTAN. 1985 (£1.50)
*74. *Liberalisation for Faster Economic Growth* HERBERT GIERSCH. 1986 (£1.50)
75. *Unemployment and the Labour Market* TOM WILSON. 1987 (£3.00)
*76. *Mr Hammond's Cherry Tree: The Morphology of Union Survival* BEN ROBERTS. 1987 (£1.50)
77. *Beyond the Welfare State* RALPH HARRIS. 1988 (£2.00)
78. *Economics Through the Looking Glass* MARK BLAUG. 1988 (£3.50)

*Wincott Memorial Lectures